MEMORIES OF
Burnopfield
DOROTHY RAND & GEORGE NAIRN

Published by
COUNTY DURHAM BOOKS

Cover - The driver of the Co-op butcher's cart and his young assistant would never imagine that their photograph would become the cover of a book.

Acknowledgments

We would like to thank the following contributors:
Beamish Photographic Archive
M Barrass
I Hair
D Hall
W McKie
B Milburn
C Smith and the late SV Walton

ISBN 1-897585-54-5

Introduction

I discovered history when I was six years old and living at 52, Busty Bank, Burnopfield. My Bedroom window faced the West Wood of the Gibside Estate and stories about the families who lived there fascinated me, starting a lifelong obsession with history, particularly local history.

Burnopfield had grown from small settlements at Sheephill and Bryans Leap. Busty Bank was on the route of an old wagonway and named after the Busty Seam which had outcropped onto the road.

Our block of three houses was built on the site of former miners cottages, and Busty Bank Quarry was in the back garden.

Next door was Union Cottage, dated 1831. The back of the house had been a dairy with a cross engraved into the flagstones of the floor, this room may have been used as a place of worship.

A relic of the 1939-45 war was just below Leap Mill Farm on the road to Rowlands Gill. A tree

trunk had been strategically placed on the side of the road, to be put in place as a road block in case of German invasion - history was all around.

Our childhood memories are the most vivid. The picture to the left was taken in 1947, the snow was higher than our living room windows. Winters were much longer and harder with roads at Byermoor and Hobson often impassable. The outside toilets at school were sometimes frozen, as was the school milk.

Dad regularly had a ton of "free" coals tipped on the road, all to be shovelled into buckets to be carried up the steps and round to the coalhouse, our Triplex range had to be blackleaded.

Most of our shopping was done at the Co-op and several Co-op delivery vans came round. Others came too including the oil man from Annfield Plain with his horse and cart and Tommy Lowes Travelling Shop which was an old bus. George Scotts butchers boy delivered our meat twice weekly, in a basket on his bicycle. We had our shoes repaired by Mr. Rush in his hut near George Scott.

Sounds are remembered - always the engine pulling trucks along the line, the waterfall at Leap Mill and the incessant barking of neighbour Minnie Milburns show collies. Once a year we could hear the band playing after the Gala and the Grove Chapel portable organ on Anniversary Sundays.

The smell of the Chapel at Harvest Festival was wonderful, also the Flower Show tents. Bells Home Bakery and the Dene Fisheries produced mouthwatering smells, and Maughans pies were famous.

Tommy Hudspiths shop was a magnet, he sold Eldorado ice cream and we loved his home-made penny ice lollies, the bright blue spearmint one was my favourite. I bought several Mars bars the first day sweets were off ration - so many memories.

'Memories of Burnopfield' has been produced as a joint effort with George Nairn who has turned his hobby of postcard collecting into a small business called "Picture the Past". My family photographs and memories along with postcards from George's extensive collection form the backbone of this book, supported by contributions from friends.

This book - one of a series published by County Durham Books - does not attempt to be a history of Burnopfield. It is a collection of photographs, facts and memories which give a flavour of how the present has grown out of the past. Most of these photographs have not been published before and we hope that you will enjoy the pictures and the memories

DOROTHY A RAND & GEORGE NAIRN

Foreword

I recall reading a book entitled "Words on Hope" an extract from which said "Today id the first day of the rest of your life" - in other words, the past has gone forever.

It is with this quote in mind that I stress how important it is that memories from the past should be recorded, in whatever form, be it spoken, written or in pictorial form so that they can be conserved for posterity.

Sadly, for whatever reasons, this has seldom been done, particularly with regard to local history and tragically, much has gone unrecorded and has been lost forever.

Mindful of this therefore, I welcome with great enthusiasm this pictorial and factual contribution by Dorothy and George to the historical archives of life in Burnopfield during the 20th century. I have no doubt that it will create much interest and recall memories from the past for many and engender discussions for the older generation, but more importantly perhaps is that it will encourage others to do likewise, particularly the younger generation so that, in time, their own memories will also be recorded and preserved ad infinitum.

On a personal note as an addicted life-long historian, I congratulate the two authors and wish them well with this publication.

JOE WALKER JP.,F.Inst.L.Ex.
County Councillor - Dipton and Burnopfield Division
1985-to date

GREETINGS FROM BURNOPFIELD.

Many of the photographs in this book are taken from postcards, which were a popular and quick means of communication, even within ones own village, at a time when the telephone was not in general use. This Thompson multiview card was used to convey New Year greetings. The top left picture shows a familiar sight from my childhood - the engine pulling the trucks along the line above the village.

A LOVELY PLACE.

This Auty card dating from before 1910, shows the view over part of the village, also the colliery rows and Catholic church at Byermoor. The sender who was staying at Mountsett wrote of Burnopfield to her parents "It is the most lovely place I have ever seen, I have been here several times".

BUSTY BANK AND SHEEPHILL.

I bought this card from Mr McCoach at Burnopfield Post Office in 1960. In the centre of the picture are two parallel hawthorn hedges showing the route of the "Coggly Bend" a narrow cobbled path which was a short cut from Burn Crook to Sheephill. In the eighteenth century weavers at Burn Crook made willow baskets for use in the coal mines. The large field on the right belonged to the Co-op, I remember "sledging" down the steep slope of the field on flattened cardboard boxes. The delayed 1953 Coronation sports were held here.

THE SPURR FAMILY.

When the coal mines developed in County Durham there was an influx of labour from other less prosperous parts of the country. The Spurr family came from the declining tin-mining area of Cornwall in the 1870's. My great-grandfather Albert James Spurr is shown here in 1891 with his family, they lived at Crookbank Cottages. Albert was a staunch Methodist, known as "Good little Albert". When news of the birth of his first child reached him in the pit, he fell on his knees and thanked God. That child was my grandfather, standing next to his mother, he was John William Spurr. The year after this photograph was taken he left school at the age of twelve to work down the pit, and so help support the still increasing family. Albert died in 1897 aged 40.

A HARD LIFE

Like many other people at that time, my grandfather, Jack Spurr had a hard life. He was forced to leave school at twelve to help support his family, he was intelligent and could have gone into one of the professions. He spent all of his working life at Byermoor Colliery, much of it as a hewer and recalled working in seams of 13 inches. He is shown here, home from the pit in 1930's outside 12 Myrtle Grove, Leazes. His careworn face reflects his tiredness. He died in 1949 of, the family thought, pneumoconiosis, but the death certificate said "Emphysema". There was no compensation for his second wife Maud, who because she was under 50, became a "ten-shilling widow" and was forced to work despite her heart problems.

Inset: My grandfather's lodge token, his initials are punched into the reverse.

BYERMOOR COLLIERY FIRST AID TEAM 1953

In hazardous occupations such as mining it is important to have trained people on the spot to give first aid and prevent further injury. A First Aid class started in 1903 in Burnopfield after a miner sustained a simple fracture of his leg in a pit accident. By the time he reached medical help it had become a compound fracture.

Front row, left to right: C. Mills, Manager of Byermoor Colliery, Sir Myers Wayman (Durham County Commissioner for St. John Ambulance Brigade) and Major Nicholson (President of the Burnopfield Division).

Back row: A Robson, J. Bainbridge, E. Gibson, W. McKie and C. Melcalf. Charlie Metcalf was awarded the St. John Life Saving Medal in 1966 for risking his own life to give morphia to his friend and colleague Billy McKie, badly injured and trapped by a serious fall of stone.

A VIEW FROM CROOKGATE

R. Johnston and Son of Gateshead produced many local cards in their "Monarch" series, often numbered in the bottom left corner. This view, posted in 1937, shows the level crossing at Crookgate, Grove Terrace and the Co-op buildings. Doctor Miller's Surgery was at 7 Grove Terrace. Former patients remember affectionately the miraculous effect of his home-made powders, the long wait on straight-backed monks settles, the old oil paintings and classical music playing on the Third Programme. Neither Dr. Miller nor Dr. Boland seemed to hurry their home visits.

GROVE TERRACE METHODIST CHURCH AND THE SMITHY

The UMC or Free Church (known as Grove Terrace Methodist Church after Union in 1932) was opened in 1870 at a cost of over £600, and enlarged in 1902. It is shown here on a photograph sold by B.C. Barkus, Burnopfield Stationery Emporium. The Sunday School rooms beneath the Chapel were used as a Welfare Clinic from the 1920's. Nothing has ever matched the taste of that Welfare Orange Juice. In 1949 I went to the Clinic on a pre-school visit. Nurse Tully invited me to take some Smarties from the jar on the table and promptly injected my unsuspecting, outstreched arm! The Smithy at the top of Busty Bank was of vital importance to the village in the days of horse-drawn vehicles.

BUSTY BANK, BURNOPFIELD. 1339.

A POSTCARD FROM HOME.

The holes in this card were made when my grandfather pinned it up in his RAMC barracks in Kent in 1916. It was sent from 40 Sheep Hill by his sister-in-law Barbara Herdman. The Billiard Hall next to the Grand was where he had won the first prize of a clock in 1898. My grandfather courted my grandmother Annie Herdman when she worked in the bakery and newsagents shop belonging to her uncle, this was above the house with the whitened steps. The shop later became Herdman and McKie, then Maughans, and more recently was owned by Alan Hall.

The Grand was a popular place for courting couples! I vividly remember queueing, along with half of Burnopfield, to see "A Queen is Crowned" in 1953.

WALTER WILLSON'S AND JOHN HAIR

These shops at 10 and 11 Busty Bank are shown about 1950. Walter Willson, famous for Smiling Service, advertised in the 1936 Parish Magazine "Good food is half the battle, get it at Walter Willsons". John Hair's business in the former Cobbler's shop started quietly in 1945. Belle Hair recollects that the rent was ten shillings a week and the first week's takings amounted to sixpence! John had to leave the RAF because he had TB, and so qualified for a loan of £100 which was used to stock the shop. When £75 had been repaid SSAFA did not want the remaining £25. Hairs had repaid their loan regularly, not one other recipient had paid back a penny. The shop sold, amongst other things, electrical and fancy goods, decorating materials and bicycles. Our first television came from there, a Cossor with a twelve inch screen, bought just before the 1953 Coronation.

THE CO-OP

The Co-op buildings dominate Burnopfield, most people shopped at "the Store" so as to earn dividend. When a member made a purchase it was written on a check with the members number - ours was 2888. Dividend Days were exciting, members from Burnopfield and other branches queued up the stairs leading to the Store Office to collect their money then went to see what was in the Dividend Sale. Many members had souvenir jubilee trays from 1939. The Co-op was built in 1889 and this photograph shows the impressive row of shops not long after completion.

DELIVERY AND TRANSPORT VEHICLES

Horse-drawn vehicles abounded in the early twentieth century. The Co-op had delivery carts with a range of goods to help the busy housewife tied to her home by housework and a large family. Heavy goods such as the large quantities of flour needed for baking were best delivered.

Most people walked long distances, a relation regularly walked from Kyo to Burnopfield and back, doing her crochet work at the same time! Horses and traps were used for certain journeys. After a trip to Newcastle by train, shoppers were glad of a ride up the bank from Rowlands Gill to Burnopfield. Bob Davidson used this photograph of his horse and trap as a Christmas 1909/New year 1910 greetings card.

CO-OP STAFF

Grocery staff (Dickie Brown is second from the left) pose outside their department. Their overalls were necessary as most foodstuffs were delivered in bulk and had to be weighed and packaged. The best Danish Butter came in barrels and had to be cut up into pounds or half pounds. I still have some barrel hoops I begged to make an old-fashioned paper-covered mistletoe for Christmas. Dried fruit and sugar were weighed out into appropriately coloured bags. I loved to watch the system of overhead cash carriers taking money to the cashier. Note the graffiti on the stone pillar

HAVING A GOOD TIME
The staff of Burnopfield Co-op are shown here on a weekend trip to Blackpool in the 1950's. On Race Wednesdays there were day trips to places such as Morecambe and Scarborough. Dickie Brown, the original owner of this photograph is second from left in the back row, how many faces can you remember?

BURNOPFIELD HALL. 1265.

BURNOPFIELD HOUSE

Also known as Burnopfield Hall, this building dates from 1720. It was built by William Newton, coalowner, his daughter and heiress had the misfortune to marry the Irish fortune hunter, Andrew Robinson Stoney. His maltreatment of her contributed to her early death, he went on to marry Mary Eleanor Bowes of Gibside and became known as Stoney Bowes. The Watson family occupied the house for about a hundred years from 1830 onwards. Dr. Robert Stirling was murdered at Rowlands Gill in 1855 while working as assistant surgeon to Doctor Watson.

THE WAR MEMORIAL

The cenotaph, situated opposite Burnopfield House in the heart of the village, was funded by the work of Burnopfield and District War Memorial Committee as a memorial to those who died in the 1914-18 war. It was unveiled on the 29th January 1921 and is still the focus of Remembrance Day tributes.

MEMORIES OF SCHOOL

Burnopfield National School was opened in 1873 at a cost of £850, Miss Gill is shown here with her class in 1917, Jenny Brewis, later Potts is at the left end of the front row. My mother, Ena May Spurr, later Noble is second from the right in the back row.

When I started school in 1949 my first headmaster was kindly Mr. Lamb, who was also local correspondent for the "Stanley News". He always greeted ladies, including myself as a teenager, by raising his hat to them. He was succeeded by Mr. Morgan.

BURNOPFIELD METHODIST CHURCH

John Wesley first preached at Burnopfield in 1746. His subsequent visits to preach at Sheephill were marked by the unveiling of the John Wesley Memorial there on Wesley Day in 1961. The first church was built in 1775 and rebuilt as Haswell Memorial Methodist Church in 1880, now it is awaiting another rebuilding. My mother was carried to Sunday School as a baby in arms - her father was Sunday School Superintendent. My grandfather's brothers - A.J. Spurr & Henry Spurr and their wives are commemorated in the Spurr Memorial Windows. A.J. Spurr (Jimmy) and his wife Martha were the first couple to be married in the church after it was licensed for marriages. They received a Bible from the Trustees on June 10th 1911.

BURNOPFIELD BOYS BRIGADE

The Boys Brigade was founded by William Alexander Smith in Glasgow in 1883 with the motto of "Sure and Stedfast", the object of the Boys Brigade was the advancement of Christ's Kingdom amongst boys. Activities included drill, competing for badges, playing in the band and going to annual camp, as well as attending Bible Class or Sunday School. Uniformed youth organisations were very popular between the wars. The 15th North West Durham Company (Burnopfield) met at Burnopfield Methodist Church, the Minister on this 1940's photograph is the Rev. J.P. Ellis.

A CORONATION IN BURNOPFIELD

Burnopfield Women's Institute held their own Coronation in 1953 with beautiful costumes made by Jenny Potts. Left to right: Cissie Fairlamb, Lily Nixon, Nancy Herdman, Dora Bell, Belle Hair, Jenny Anderson (kneeling), Belle Brown, Nellie Heslop and Millie Brown.

HASWELL MEMORIAL METHODIST CHURCH YOUTH CLUB.

The social activities provided by churches and chapels are an important part of village life. The Youth Club is shown here about 1962. Back row, left to right: John Herdman, Bernard Reay, Alan Burns, Dorothy Noble, Derek Kemp, Joan Smith, Margaret Beckham, Jack Peacock. Front Row: Alan Watson, Joan Nicholson, Joan Herdman, Rev. John Robinson, Cynthia Bird, Doreen Scott, Alan Herdman.

THE MERRY OPTOMISTS

This well-known group of entertainers was based in the Wesley Hall, they gave performances there and in neighbouring villages. They are shown here in 1939, members included Nan and Norman Seth, Walter John Churcher, Elsie Churcher, Bertha Davis and Jenny and Harold Potts. The photograph was taken by Stephen Young from Shield Row, he was called upon to photograph other local groups in the 1930's.

THE SONS OF TEMPERANCE

This organisation was a Friendly Society and Temperance Order. Every member had to sign a pledge of total abstinence at a time when the "Demon Drink" blighted the happiness of many families. Funds were raised by entrance fees, fines and contributions to pay out sickness and funeral benefits. Temperance Orders were supported by the churches, particularly the Methodists. Officials of the Burnofield Rising Star Division are shown here, including three members of the Spurr family. My great-uncle Jim Spurr is on the extreme left, he was well-known as a local preacher and was active in other areas of public life. One hundred and nineteen members served in the Great War and another fifteen made the Supreme Sacrifice as recorded on a Roll of Honour.

THE OPENING OF THE AMBULANCE STATION

In 1903 local miners requested a First Aid Class which Doctor Boland held in his own home. This Ambulance Association grew rapidly and in 1907 it was decided to register as a Division of St. John Ambulance Brigade the first in County Durham. £300 was needed to build an Ambulance Station with a house for a horse van (supplied by Sir William Angus for £95), and an operating room. This was raised by door-to-door collections, a levy of 1d a week from miners, and from donations. The Burns Pit disaster of February 1909 emphasised the need and accelerated the rate of donations. Mrs Watson of Burnopfield House donated the site for the Ambulance Station, and on 14th August 1909 Miss Mabel Watson officially opened the building. She received a beautiful gold key in return. This Ambulance Station was the first of its kind in the North of England, it was built by Mr Davis of Burnopfield.

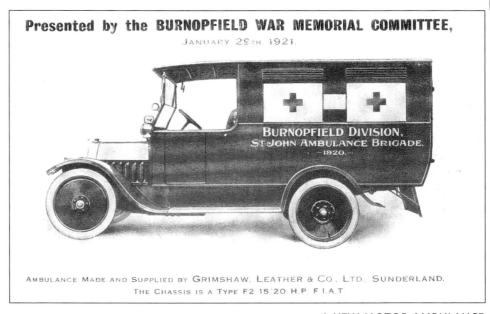

A NEW MOTOR AMBULANCE

The horse-drawn ambulance van bought in 1909 could only be used when an approved horse of at least 15.2 hands could be found at the Co-op, collieries, livery stables or from local tradesmen. The van was well used both after accidents and for planned journeys to and from the RVI. Non-subscribers paid for each journey and funding for the Ambulance Station and van was, until 1914 provided by annual sports and a flower show. In August 1911 while the Ambulance Sports were being held a message came about the charabanc disaster on Medomsley Bank. The Ambulance Brigade answered the call, they manhandled the heavy wooden ambulance out of the field and down three miles of rough roads to deal with the dead, dying and injured, leaving word for a horse to be brought later.

In 1921 the Burnopfield Brigade received a new motor ambulance, the inscription plate said "This motor ambulance is the gift of the Burnopfield and District War Memorial Committee to the Burnopfield Division of the St John Ambulance Brigade as a token of appreciation of the men who gave their services and as a memorial to those who gave their lives in the European War 1914-1918". The horse-drawn van was then sold for £20 and the upkeep of the new ambulance was helped by the sale of hundreds of copies of this postcard at one penny each. In 1948 the National Health Service bought this van.

GOING TO THE LEAZES

This Card, posted in 1911 clearly shows the state of the roads and evidence of horse-drawn traffic. The square building on the right was used as a Branch Library. I joined the library when I was seven, Miss Tiplady was in charge and strict silence was observed. The Black Horse public house can just be seen beyond it, before the entrance to The Fold. In the 1960's a new house was built near here made of stone from old houses in the vicinity. One old house had a carved lintel over the fireplace with the inscription 16 IH 69 'J.H.' was probably one of the Harrison family who owned this land in the seventeenth century. The old malt house was demolished in 1960 and rough hewn oak beams were found buried in chaff.

FRONT STREET, BURNOPFIELD. 1202

LOOKING BACK

On the extreme right of the picture is Forsters Shop, even in 1936 it advertised as R.F. Forster (The Old Firm). In the 1950's Eddie Forster was the proprietor. Beyond the Sun Inn next door is a board advertising The Derwent Pavilion which was behind it. There was entertainment of various kinds here - films and "Go as you please". At the time of this photograph seats were 2d, 4d and 6d.

COLIN MILBURN 1941-1990
Colin's talent in playing cricket showed itself early when he played with his friends in the back street, he made his first appearance for Burnopfield Cricket Club at the age of twelve. He went on to play for Chester-le-Street, Northamptonshire and England. I always remember him as a beaming, affable person. Tom Graveney said of him "Colin Milburn was one of the great characters of cricket and brought fun and entertainment to this wonderful game, both on and off the field. I know that when his name is mentioned, it puts a smile on all our faces."

THE LEAZES, BURNOPFIELD. 1260.

A TEMPERANCE HALL AND A PUBLIC HOUSE

On the left is the Church Hall, the notice says "Church Institute". This started life as the Temperance Hall, built by the Lintzford Band of Hope in 1872. It was later presented to the Church by Miss Allgood for the use of parishioners. Beyond the adjacent houses and shops is "The Travellers Rest". In my childhood it was referred to as "Jack Allan's". It was once owned by Jack Allan, a famous Newcastle United centre forward of the 1930's.

LEAZES HALL

Dating from the eighteenth century, Leazes Hall has had many occupants. In the nineteenth century it was, for some years, a girls school. One occupant around the beginning of the twentieth century was William J. Handcock, Building Contractor, Timber Merchant and proprietor of the Burnopfield Sawmill which was near Haswell Methodist Chapel. Leazes Hall is now a nursing home.

ST JAMES CHURCH

The Parish of Burnopfield was carved out of the Parish of Tanfield as the growing community justified its own place of worship, St. James Church was consecrated in 1873. There were extensive centenary celebrations in 1973, including a Flower Festival and history exhibition in the Church Hall. Shown above are a souvenir postcard and envelope which could be left in a special postbox to be franked with a commemorative postmark.

LEAZES JUNIOR SCHOOL FOOTBALL XI

This successful team is shown about 1958.

Back Row, left to right: Terry Barnes, Brian Shield, Kenneth Raye, Alan Herdman, John McKie, Ian Tallentire, George Browell. Front Row: Billy Shaw, Alan Proud, Alan Watson, Bobby Irving, Ernest Welch.

The 1957-58 team were West Stanley District Junior Schools Football League Champions and Shimeld Cup Winners.

BURNOPFIELD SILVER BAND

There were many social activities earlier in the century. A popular sight and sound was the Burnopfield Silver Band shown here in 1925. A young Nat Herdman stands proudly with his cornet outside 15 Eden Avenue, the details of his uniform can be clearly seen.

JUDGING A LEEK SHOW
Dickie Brown (with the cigarette) and Jack Bell are concentrating on the task in hand and are oblivious to the camera. It was - and still is - a matter of great pride to have grown prizewinning produce.

These distinctive trees at Bryan's Leap Farm were for many years a familiar feature of the view over the valley until struck by lightning.

LAUNDRY AT THE LEAZES

This photograph was taken at 12 Myrtle Grove in the 1930's. Even though progress had been made from poss-tub to washer it was still hard work. The agitator on this Ewbank washer was activated by vigorously turning the handle. More elbow grease was needed to turn the wringer.

HOBSON COLLIERY

Hobson Colliery was officially Burnopfield Colliery. The first shaft was sunk here in 1725 and the original village dates from that time - two long streets of stone-built houses, with other streets behind. In the 1890's the annual output was 140,000 tons. By 1902 Hobson Colliery was supplying electricity. Before nationalisation Hobson was owned and worked by John Bowes and Partners and it closed in 1968.

PREPARING FOR WAR AT HOBSON

Hobson people - members of St. John Ambulance and others - practiced First Aid for the 1939-45 war. Many precautions were taken, there was a Cleansing Station set up at Pickering Nook to deal with cases of contamination but fortunately it was never needed.

THE GIBSIDE ESTATE

This postcard, showing the hunt in front of Gibside Hall was sent to a baby called Olive for her first birthday in 1915. Land girls were billeted in the servants quarters in the 1914-18 war. A South Shields solicitor, Victor Grunhut rented Gibside Hall for a few years from 1908, he has used this photograph of himself on horseback in front of the Hall for his 1911 Christmas card.

A ROYAL VISIT

The Rev. Frederick H. Britton was the 10th Vicar of Burnopfield and Lord Strathmore's Chaplain at Gibside. On Tuesday 23rd June 1964 H.M. Queen Elizabeth the Queen Mother paid a private and informal visit to Gibside before the Chapel was placed in the care of the National Trust. She enjoyed tea on the lawn at the gamekeeper's cottage which had been furnished with a new staircarpet and loo for the occasion! Before she left, the Queen Mother posed for this photograph:

Left to right: Mrs Britton, Col. E.H. Kirkup (Lord Strathmore's Agent), H.M. Queen Elizabeth, the Queen Mother, Rev. F.H. Britton and Mrs Kirkup.

In July 1966 the Queen Mother attended a service to mark the restoration of Gibside Chapel by the National Trust.

BURNOPFIELD SHOW

The show attracted crowds from surrounding towns and villages and in the 1950's and 1960's I remember the excitement of the previous week when the "hoppings" arrived. The day itself was a long one, our carefully prepared exhibits had to be in place and ready for judging by 10.00am. Then it was home for something to eat and back to the show for the rest of the day. We went first to the tents to see if any of the family had won prizes for flowers and vegetables, baking, handicrafts or floral art. There were many attractions during the afternoon and evening. Decorated pit ponies and tradesmens carts were paraded and sheep, pigs and cattle were judged. There might be a dog show, a sheaf throwing contest and gymkhana. Prize money was paid out between 5pm and 6pm. I once spent mine on a yellow blouse which I'd seen in the Baby Shop window.

Burnopfield Flower Show, thought to be the oldest in North-West Durham, started in 1873 at the suggestion of Mr. Twizell, gardener to Miss Surtees of Hamsterley Hall. An Agricultural Section was added in 1921 and in 1932 a Great Band Contest was held. The Diamond Jubilee Show of 1933 was opened by Sir Arthur and Lady Lambert. Here the crowd watches Scottish Dancing at one of the last shows to be held in Burnopfield.

RIPPON FOUNTAIN. BURNOPFIELD.   1259.

THE RIPPON FOUNTAIN

This brown marble fountain was erected on the steep bank into the village from Rowlands Gill, to refresh both man and beast. It is inscribed: "Erected by Miss M.A. Rippon in remembrance of her brother William C. Rippon, of his life's residence in Burnopfield, and in kindness to dumb animals 1906. The Donor of this fountain died 3rd October before its completion".

Many years ago an amusement wagon carrying Lowdon's Electric Jumping Horses back to Winlaton from Burnopfield Flower Show crashed through the fence below the fountain. It was saved by a tree from falling into the Dene culvert.

OLD MILL, BURNOPFIELD. "Auty Series." G.H., W.B. 1382.

LEAP MILL FARM

There has been a watermill on this site for at least 250 years. In the middle of the nineteenth century there was also a naphtha manufactory. The cottage connected with this (now demolished) is nearest to the camera on this pre-1910 postcard. Later there was also a charcoal manufactory. The corn mill was not used after the late 1920's. The waterwheel disintegrated due to rust and woodworm, but a replacement wheel was installed a few years ago, as part of a programme of restoration. In 1869 a self-acting hydraulic ram was installed beside the farm to pump the pure spring water up into the village, prior to this the women of the village had to carry the water up the steep bank.

LAST LOAD HOME

Local children liked to "help" the farmer at Leap Mill. We were captured on film in 1955 and this photograph won 10 shillings in a "Happy Snapshot" competition in the "Stanley News". The farmer is Ben Turnbull, who has his arm around my shoulder. Next to me is June Blatchford my next door neighbour. The boy is Ian Robinson who lived in the farm cottage.

GOODBYE

A picture to make you smile as we come to the end of this book of memories of Burnopfield. We hope that you have found it interesting and have recalled many happy memories of your own.